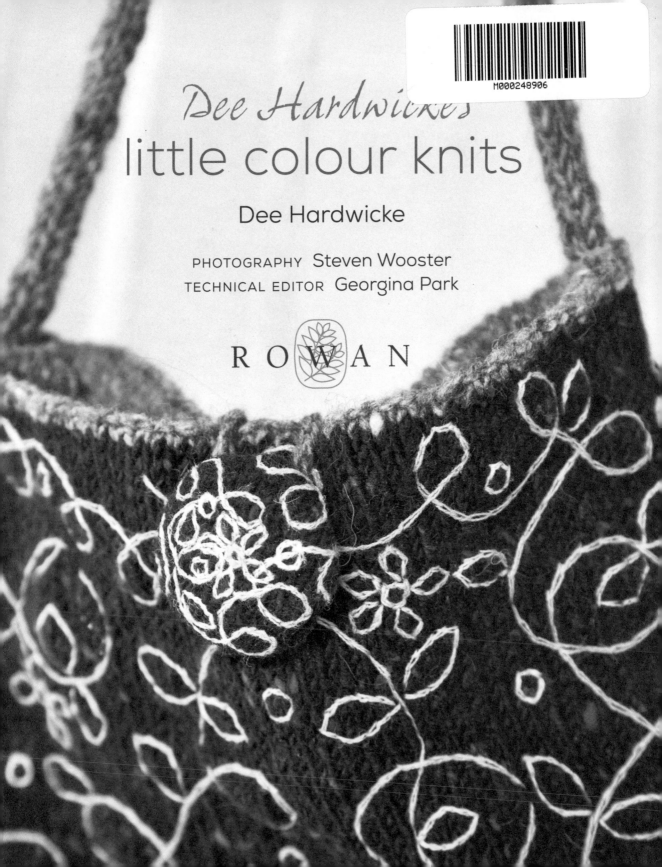

Dee Hardwicke's
little colour knits

Dee Hardwicke

PHOTOGRAPHY Steven Wooster
TECHNICAL EDITOR Georgina Park

ROWAN

Dee Hardwicke's Little Colour Knits
First published in 2013 by
Rowan Yarns
Green Lane Mill
Holmfirth
HD9 2DX

Created and produced by
Berry & Co (Publishing) Ltd
47 Crewys Road
Childs Hill
London NW2 2AU

Design Anne Wilson
Pattern checking Jill Gray
Editor Katie Hardwicke
Charts Anne Wilson
Styling Susan Berry

British LIbrary Cataloguing in Publication Data
A catalogue record of this book is available from the
British Library

ISBN 978-1-907544-62-0
Printed in Singapore

contents

introduction

As an artist I am always exploring new designs and my inspiration comes from the natural landscape. My studio is in the historic market town of Monmouth, where I am surrounded by the beauty of the Welsh Marches. I am inspired by leaves, flowers, seedlings... all these things are around me and attract me in different ways at different times of the year.

At some seasons, it is the pure colour that catches my attention: vibrant reds, glinting golds or earthy browns in autumn, or the fresh greens, sharp blues and citrus yellows of spring. At other times, it is the stark outline of shape and form.

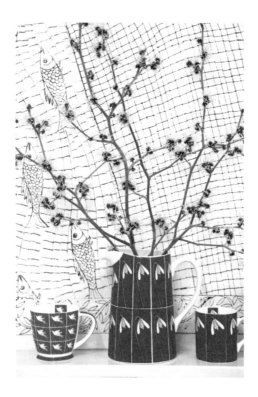 

While ceramics are my first love, in recent years I have enjoyed expanding my design horizons and a couple of years ago started to translate some of my motifs onto paper and packaging. I have always had a love for yarns, and having knitted with Rowan yarns and patterns it wasn't long before I began to wonder what would happen when my motifs were translated in knitted form.

With the help of Georgina Park, whose knit and design experience made her the perfect partner, we began to develop my initial charts into patterns and explore which of my other motifs could be translated into stitch. Rowan yarns, with their great range of colours, seemed another perfect partner.

introduction

motif inspiration

I have always responded creatively to my surroundings and the changing seasons. Everything starts life in my sketchbook, each intricately painted page illustrates the textures, colours and images of the rich landscape that surrounds my home, nestled between the Black Mountains and Brecon Beacons.

I work in several mediums including pencil, watercolour, and pen and ink. I sometimes make notes and record memories alongside the images. These sketches and paintings are the basis for all of my work.

The next stage when working on a new project, whether it is ceramics, stationery or knitting, is to translate the artwork to suit the medium that I am using. Sometimes that might be a single image and other times it might be creating a pattern from one. The shape, feel and colours of the original artwork will lend themselves to different interpretations. In this book for example, the

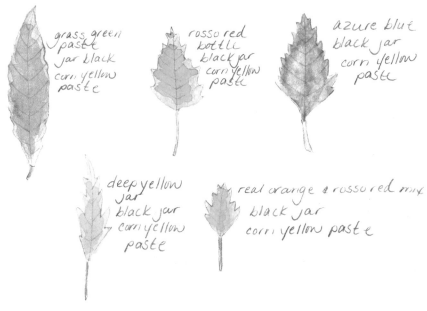

1. yellow mix - mix as 5'
2. orange - liquid - strong mix
3 black jar
4. plain slip - background

pearl-bordered fritillary
male

1. yellow mix - mix 125 - thinly
2. orange liquid - strong mix - thin wash
3 yellow paste
4 orange paste
5 black jar
6 white paste
7. plain slip - background

pearl-bordered fritillary

underside ~ male

1. white paste
2. plain slip
3 yellow paste
4. black jar

marbled white

1. corn yellow paste
2. white paste
3. med blue - thick
4. orange - thick mix
5 plain slip

butterflies
seen in garden
and countryside

painted lady

Oak Leaf cushion (see page 12) was directly suggested by the oak leaf ceramic tiles (above). The embroidery on the Clematis bag (see page 22) drew its inspiration from an amalgam of the swirling shapes of leaf, flower and fruit watercolours (opposite) and the Butterfly patchwork and purse (see page 18) came directly from my first sketches of different butterflies (see page 9).

motif inspiration

oak leaf cushion

This cushion uses one of my favourite motifs, the oak leaf. It figures in many of my ceramic pieces and is an eternally popular design. I have chosen to work it in three rich colours in a cosy, soft yarn. You can make the cushion back from fabric or create a plain knitted version using one of the colours used for the front. Allow an extra ball of yarn in that colour if so. Like the Seedling cushion on page 24, it is worked using the intarsia technique. If you like the design, it would be easy to work it up into a bigger cushion or a small throw, for example. In a thick yarn like *Lima*, it will knit up quite quickly.

oak leaf cushion

spring
hot
water
bottle
cover

There is nothing like snuggling up with a hot water bottle in
a cosy cover on a cold night! Rowan's *Felted Tweed DK is* the
perfect yarn for the job, as it is soft and warm, comes in a lovely
range of colours and knits up quickly. This is a design classic
based on my leaf motif in cool greys and greens.

spring lace shawl

I just love the diaphanous effect of lace and find a lacy pattern really absorbing to knit. Rowan's *Fine Lace* yarn proved the ideal yarn to knit this design, as it is delicate yet warm and soft, too. I made this little shawl quite small but there is nothing to stop you from working a much longer one or even one that is wider. Just add more repeats of the lace motif and remember that you will need more yarn if working a bigger design.

spring lace shawl

butterfly
purse

This little butterfly design, knitted in Rowan's *Felted Tweed DK*, was inspired by some of my drawings of butterlies, which appeal to me greatly, as I love their delicate shapes and soft colours. The tubular handle is knitted on double pointed needles, but you could just as easily make the tubing on a large knitting dolly. If you like the butterfly design, why not use it for a cushion (like the oak leaf design) or even a throw, mixed with similar-sized rectangles in plain colours (see page 64)?

butterfly purse

reindeer runner and tile coasters

I love the cool blues and greys of this design, which looks very elegant and Scandinavian with simple china and crystal glasses. It is knitted in two colours of Rowan *Fine Tweed*. The accompanying coasters, knitted using the border pattern, add a nice finishing touch.

clematis bag

This little bag, inspired by clematis vine drawings in my sketchbook, has a lovely, delicate appeal with its scrolling embroidery covering the whole bag. It is knitted in two colours of Rowan *Fine Tweed* and fastened with a striking button, made from a button kit, covered in a knitted fabric that is also embroidered in the same style as the bag.

clematis bag

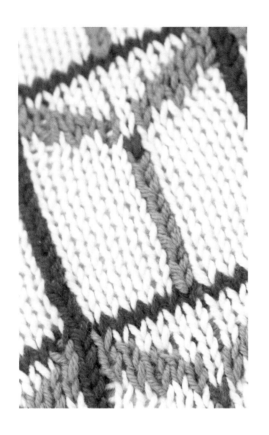

seedling cushion

I love this delicate little seedling motif and I have used it here to create a tile effect for this small cushion. I used Rowan *Wool Cotton DK* because it has such a good crisp finish that it defines the motifs really well. The single stitch in red helps to focus the eye on the graphic shape of the seedling. You could pick out the green or blue for the cushion back.

seedling cushion

tulip lace wrap and cloche hat

I knitted these in Rowan's *Baby Merino Silk DK*, which has a lovely soft and silky feel. It also showed up the texture of the tulip lace motif very well, I think. You could, if you wished, make the wrap longer than I did mine. It is a very easy lace pattern so ideal for someone who wants to try some lace knitting for the first time.

tulip lace tea cosy

Knitted in *Felted Tweed DK*, this little tea cosy has been keeping the teapot warm in my studio for my endless supply of tea when I am designing. It is knitted in two halves. If you wanted to have some fun, you could make a little bunch of the same crocheted spirals for the button loop into a little tuft to adorn the cosy top! As with all lace patterns, the cosy is slightly see through, so pick a colour for it that goes nicely with your china for maximum effect.

tulip wristwarmers

These wristwarmers, with the long cuffs and fingerless tops,
are great when you are working and need to use your hands but
they are so pretty I am inclined just to use them as an accessory.
My little tulip tiles were the inspiration for the design, which
has been translated using Rowan *Fine Tweed*. They are worked
using the intarsia technique.

oak leaf cushion

This cushion uses one of my favourite motifs, the oak leaf. It figures in many of my ceramic pieces.

finished size
Approx 30 x 30cm/12 x 12in

yarns
1 x 50g ball each of Rowan *Lima* in Amazon 879 (A), Titicaca 883 (B), La Paz 891 (C)

needles
Pair of 5.5mm (US 9) knitting needles

extras
Cushion backing fabric
30cm/12in cushion pad

tension
20 sts and 26 rows to 10cm/4in square measured over St st using 5.5mm (US 9) needles, *or size to obtain correct tension.*

abbreviations
See page 66

note
Chart is read from right to left for a right side (knit) row and from left to right for a wrong side (purl) row. Use the intarsia method for working the oak leaf patterns and grids across the chart.

front
Using 5.5mm (US 9) needles and yarn A, cast on 64 sts.
Working in St st and using colour chart as a guide, work all rows of colour chart to complete cushion front. Cast off.

making up
Block or press your cushion front as preferred, and sew in ends. With right sides together, sew cushion front and back together, remembering to insert your cushion pad before completing the fourth side if your cushion back does not contain a zip.

oak leaf cushion

KEY

■ Amazon 879 (A)

■ Titicaca 883 (B)

■ La Paz 891 (C)

spring hot water bottle cover

The simple leaf motif of my logo makes a nice addition to this elegant but warm hot water bottle cover.

finished size
Approx 21 x 34cm/8¼ x 13½in

yarns
Rowan *Felted Tweed DK*
2 x 50g balls in Clay 177 (A)
1 ball each in Carbon 159 (B) and Avocado 161 (C)

needles
Pair of 4mm (US 6) knitting needles

extras
4 buttons

tension
22 sts and 30 rows to 10cm/4in square measured over St st using 4mm (US 6) needles, *or size to obtain correct tension.*

abbreviations
See page 66

note
Chart is read from right to left for a right side (knit) row and from left to right for a wrong side (purl) row. Use the intarsia method for working the spring pattern across the chart

front (make 1)
Using 4mm (US 6) needles and yarn A, cast on 38 sts.
Row 1 (RS) Knit.
Row 2 (WS) Purl.
Working in St st throughout unless otherwise stated, increase 1 st at each end of next and following 6 alt rows, finishing with WS facing for next row. (52 sts)
Work 9 rows in St st, finishing with RS facing for next row.

Chart placement
*Next row** K6 using yarn A, using intarsia method work across row 1 of chart, k2 using yarn A, work across row 1 of chart again, knit to end using yarn A.
Next row P6 using yarn A, using intarsia method work across row 2 of chart, p2 using yarn A, work across row 2 of chart again, purl to end using yarn A.
Cont as set until all chart rows have been worked. **
Work 2 rows in St st using yarn A, then repeat from * to ** once more.
Work 6 rows in St st using yarn A, ending with RS facing for next row.

Shape top

Dec 1 st at each end of next 4 rows.
(44 sts)
Cast off 3 sts at beg of next 4 rows.
(32 sts)
Cast off 2 sts at beg of next 2 rows.
(28 sts)

Collar

Next row Using yarn A, k1, *k2, p2, rep
from * to last 3 sts, k3.
Next row P1, *p2, k2, rep from * to last 3
sts, p3.
Last 2 rows set rib.
Cont in rib as set until collar measures
15cm/6in from start of ribbing, ending
with RS facing for next row.
Cast off in rib.

lower back (make 1)

Using 4mm (US 6) needles and yarn A,
cast on 38 sts.
Row 1 (RS) Knit.
Row 2 (WS) Purl.
Working in St st throughout unless
otherwise stated, inc 1 st at each end of
next and foll 6 alt rows, finishing with WS
facing for next row. (52 sts)
Work 19 rows in St st, ending with RS
facing for next row.
Cont in rib as foll:
Next row K1, *k2, p2, rep from * to last 3
sts, k3.
Next row K1, *p2, k2, rep from * to last 3
sts, p2, k1.

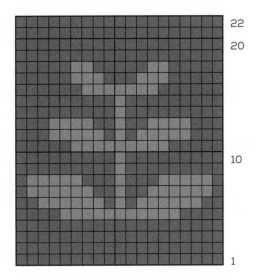

Rep last 2 rows once more.
Buttonhole row Maintaining rib patt,
work 7, yf, work 2 tog, work 10, yf, work 2
tog, work 10, yf, work 2 tog, work 10, yf,
work 2 tog, work to end.
Work 3 more rows in rib.
Cast off in rib.

upper back (make 1)

Using yarn A, cast on 52 sts.
Next row K1, *k2, p2, rep from * to last 3
sts, k3.
Next row K1, *p2, k2, rep from * to last 3
sts, p2, k1.
Rep last 2 rows 3 times more.

spring hot water bottle cover

Work 18 rows in St st, ending with RS facing for next row.

Chart placement
Next row K17 using yarn A, using intarsia method work across row 1 of chart, k16. using yarn A.

Next row P16 using yarn A, using intarsia method work across row 2 of chart, p17 using yarn A.

Cont as set until all 22 rows of chart have been worked.

At the same time, beg top shaping as detailed below after row 18 has been worked.

Shape top
Dec 1 st at each end of next 4 rows. (44 sts)

Cast off 3 sts at beg of next 4 rows. (32 sts)

Cast off 2 sts at beg of next 2 rows. (28 sts)

Collar
Next row Using yarn A, k1, *p2, k2, rep from * to last 3 sts, p2, k1.

Next row K1, *k2, p2, rep from * to last 3 sts, k3.

Last 2 rows set rib

Cont in rib as set until collar measures 15cm/6in from start of ribbing, ending with RS facing for next row.

Cast off in rib.

making up
Block or press each piece to size. Sew in ends. With wrong sides together, sew down each side of the collar for 10cm/4in. Turn work inside out, and complete side and lower edge seams, overlapping upper and lower backs by the ribbing, and making sure that the lower back edges are sandwiched between the front and upper back edges when sewing together. Turn right side out and sew buttons onto upper back, using buttonholes as a guide.

spring lace shawl

With this delicate scarf I used the leaf motif again but translated it this time into a lovely lace pattern. Rowan *Fine Lace* did the job perfectly!

finished size

Approx 40 x 110cm/15½ x 43¼in

yarn

3 x 50g balls of Rowan *Fine Lace* in Patina 924

needles

Pair of 3mm (US 2) knitting needles

tension

32 sts and 42 rows to 10cm/4in square measured over patt using 3mm (US 2) needles, *or size to obtain correct tension.*

abbreviations

See page 66

to make

Using 3mm (US 2) needles and contrasting waste thread, cast on 124 sts.

shawl body

Row 1 (RS) Knit.
Row 2 (WS) Purl.
Row 3 K2, *k8, k2tog, yo, ssk, k8. Rep from * 5 times more, k2.
Row 4 P2, *p7, p2tog, drop the yo off needle, [yo] twice, p2tog, p7. Rep from * 5 times more, p2.
Row 5 K2, *k6, k2tog, drop yos off needle, [yo] 3 times, ssk, k6. Rep from * 5 times more, k2.
Row 6 P2, *p5, p2tog, drop yos off needle, [yo] 4 times, p2tog, p5. Rep from * 5 times

more, p2.
Row 7 K2, *k4, k2tog, drop yos off needle, [yo] 5 times, ssk, k4. Rep from * 5 times more, k2.
Row 8 P2, *p3, p2tog, drop yos off needle, [yo] 5 times, p2tog, p3. Rep from * 5 times more, p2.
Row 9 K2, *k2, k2tog, drop yos off left-hand needle, turn and cast on 6 sts, turn again and slide the right-hand needle under 6 dropped strands, yrn and knit back under dropped strands, yo, slide right-hand needle under newly wrapped strands again, yrn and knit back under dropped strands, turn and cast on 6 sts, turn again, ssk, k2. Rep from * 5 times more, k2
Row 10 P2, *p9, p2tog, p10. Rep from * 5 times more, p2.
Row 11 K2, *k8, k2tog, yo, ssk, k8. Rep from * 5 times more, k2.
Row 12 P2, *p7, p2tog, drop the yo off needle, [yo] twice, p2tog, p7. Rep from * 5 times more, p2.
Row 13 K2, *k6, k2tog, drop yos off needle, [yo] 3 times, ssk, k6. Rep from * 5 times more, k2.
Row 14 P2, *p5, p2tog, drop yos off needle, [yo] 4 times, p2tog, p5. Rep from * 5 times more, p2.
Row 15 K2, *k2, k2tog, drop yos off left-hand needle, turn and cast on 4 sts, turn again and slide the right-hand needle under 4 dropped strands, yrn and knit back under dropped strands, yo, slide

right-hand needle under newly wrapped strands again, yrn and knit back under dropped strands, turn and cast on 4 sts, turn again, ssk, k2. Rep from * 5 times more, k2.

Row 16 P2, *p9, p2tog, p10. Rep from * 5 times more, p2.

Row 17 K2, *k8, k2tog, yo, ssk, k8. Rep from * 5 times more, k2.

Row 18 P2, *p7, p2tog, drop the yo off needle, [yo] twice, p2tog, p7. Rep from * 5 times more, p2.

Row 19 K2, *k2, k2tog, drop yos off left-hand needle, turn and cast on 2 sts, turn again and slide the right-hand needle under 2 dropped strands, yrn and knit back under dropped strands, yo, slide right-hand needle under newly wrapped strands again, yrn and knit back under dropped strands, turn and cast on 2 sts, turn again, ssk, k2. Rep from * 5 times more, k2.

Row 20 P2, *p9, p2tog, p10. Rep from * 5 times more, p2.

Row 21 Knit.

Row 22 Purl.

These 22 rows form the patt. Rep these 22 rows 19 times more.

Next row (RS) Knit, increasing by 6 sts evenly across the row. (130 sts)

top edge

Row 1 Purl.

Row 2 *K5, yf, sl 1, k2tog, psso, yf, k5. Rep from * to end.

Row 3 Purl.

Row 4 *K4, yf, k1, sl 1, k2tog, psso, k1, yf, k4. Rep from * to end.

Row 5 Purl.

Row 6 *K3, yf, k2, sl 1, k2tog, psso, k2, yf, k3. Rep from * to end.

Row 7 Purl.

Row 8 *K2, yf, k3, sl 1, k2tog, psso, k3, yf, k2. Rep from * to end.

Row 9 Purl.

Row 10 *K1, yf, k4, sl 1, k2tog, psso, k4, yf, k1. Rep from * to end.

Row 11 Purl.

Cast off knitwise.

bottom edge

With RS facing, carefully remove the waste thread used to cast on, picking up all 124 sts of work onto needle.

Next row (RS) Knit, inc by 6 sts evenly across the row. (130 sts)

Complete as rows 1–11 of top edge and cast off knitwise.

making up

Block or press as preferred. Sew in ends.

butterfly purse

I was itching to turn one of my butterfly sketches into a knit design and I think it is perfect for this little bag.

finished size
Approx 12 x 12cm/4¾ x 4¾in, plus handle

yarns
1 x 50g ball each of Rowan *Felted Tweed DK* in Maritime 167 (A), Celadon 184 (B), Gilt 160 (C), Treacle 145 (D)

needles
Pair of 4mm (US 6) knitting needles
2 x 4mm (US 6) double pointed needles (dpn)

extras
Stitch holders

tension
22 sts and 30 rows to 10cm/4in square measured over St st using 4mm (US 6) needles, *or size to obtain correct tension.*

abbreviations
See page 66

note
Chart is read from right to left for a right side (knit) row, and left to right for a wrong side (purl) row. Use the intarsia method for working the butterfly pattern across the chart.

bag panel (make 2)

Using 4mm (US 6) needles and yarn A, cast on 31 sts.

Beg with a knit row, work 8 rows St st.

Next row K6 using yarn A, work across row 1 of chart, k6 using yarn A.

Next row P6 using yarn A, work across row 2 of chart, p6 using yarn A.

Cont as set, until all rows of chart have been worked, ending with a WS row.

Work 5 rows St st.

Knit 3 rows.

Next row Cast off 1 st (1 st left on right-hand needle), k2, slip last 3 sts onto a stitch holder, cast off 23 sts, k2, cast off last st. **Fasten off.**

Slip last 3 sts onto a stitch holder.

making up and handle construction

With right sides together, stitch side and base of bag together, using cast-off stitches at each edge of the bag as a seam allowance. With right side facing, slip 3 sts from one panel and adjacent 3 sts for the other onto a dpn. Knit all 6 stitches. Without turning the work, slide these stitches to the opposite end of the dpn, pull yarn around the back, and knit again. Continue in this manner, knitting a tubular handle for the bag, until the handle measures 80cm/31½in from the bag top. Join working end of handle to 6 sts remaining on bag top and cast off using three-needle cast off method.

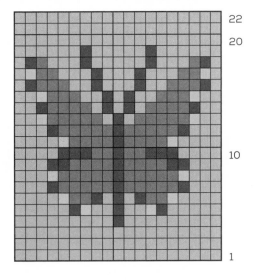

KEY

■ Maritime 167 (A)

□ Celadon 184 (B)

□ Gilt 160 (C)

■ Treacle 145 (D)

reindeer runner and tile coasters

I love reindeer designs. Worked in blue and grey, they create an elegant table runner. The checked border pattern was used to make some matching coasters. These little coasters are a great way to use up leftover yarns and a nice way to practise Fairisle knitting!

reindeer runner

finished size
Approx 30 x 180cm/12 x 70¾in

yarns
Rowan Fine Tweed
10 x 25g balls in Muker 367 (A)
3 balls in Buckden 364 (B)

needles
Pair of 3.25mm (US 3) knitting needles
3.25mm (US 3) circular needle,
150–200cm/1.5–2yd long

tension
26 sts and 38 rows to 10cm/4in square measured over St st using 3.25mm (US 3) needles, *or size to obtain correct tension.*

abbreviations
See page 66

note
Charts are read from right to left for a right side (knit) row, and left to right for a wrong side (purl) row. Use the Fairisle method for stranding the yarn across the tile border for this runner, and the intarsia method for working each reindeer.

runner body
Using 3.25mm (US 3) needles and yarn A, cast on 80 stitches.
Beg with a knit row, work rows 1–62 of chart A in St st.
Rep rows 7–60, and then rows 1–6 once more.
Using yarn A only, cont in St st until work measures 72cm/28½in from cast-on edge, ending with RS facing for next row. Work rows 1–60 of chart A once more, then rows 1–62 of chart B.
Using yarn A only, cont in St st until work measures 144cm/56¾in from cast-on edge, ending with RS facing for next row. Work rows 1–6 of chart A once, then rows 3–56 of chart B. Finally, work rows 1–62 of chart B and cast off in yarn A.

edging
*Using 3.25mm (US 3) circular needle and with RS facing, pick up and knit 456 sts down one side of the runner using

yarn A. To ensure the pattern stays correct, this equates to picking up 6 sts along each of the 6 tile borders, 84 sts along each of the three 2 x 2 reindeer panels, and 84sts along both of the 2 St st panels.

Using rows 1–6 of chart A as a guide, work 6 rows of the tile border down the edge of the table runner, making sure you start off with the appropriate yarn (i.e. yarn A if the adjacent tile is in yarn B, or yarn B if the adjacent tile is yarn A).

Cast off using yarn A.**
Rep from * to ** for the second long edge.

making up
Block or press to size as preferred. Sew in ends.

reindeer runner

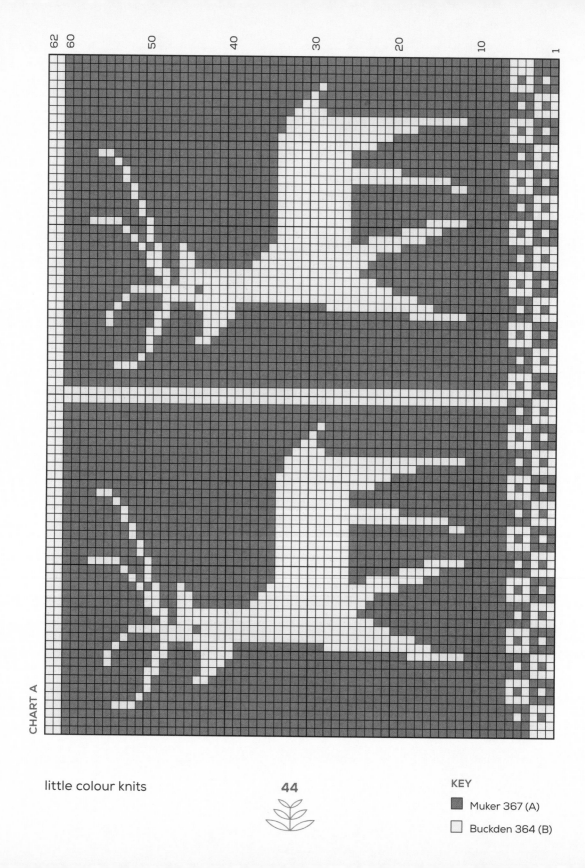

little colour knits

KEY

■ Muker 367 (A)

□ Buckden 364 (B)

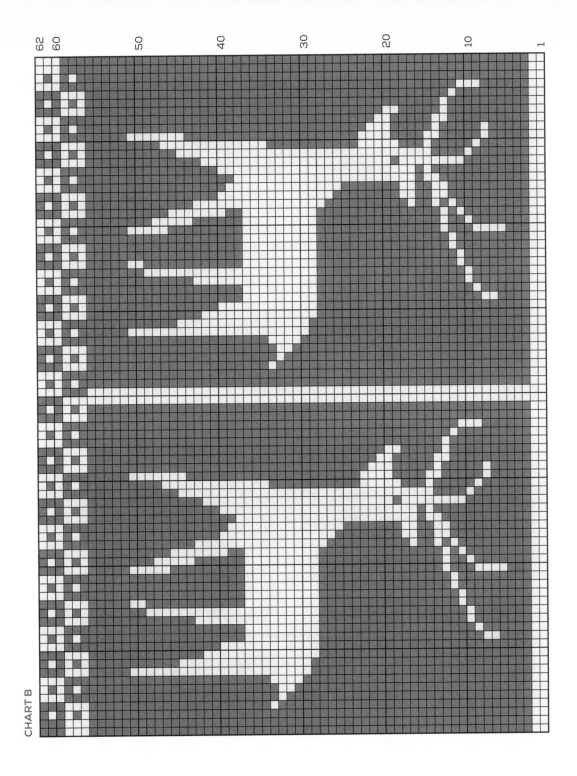

62 60 50 40 30 20 10 1

45

reindeer runner

tile coasters

finished size
Approx 10 x 10cm/4 x 4in

yarns
1 x 25g ball each of *Rowan Fine Tweed* in Muker 367(A) and Buckden 364 (B)
(1 ball of each yarn will make 4 coasters)

needles
Pair of 3.25mm (US 3) knitting needles

tension
30 sts and 30 rows to 10cm/4in square of colour worked St st approx, using 3.25mm (US 3) needles, *or size to obtain correct tension.*

abbreviations
See page 66

note
Chart is read from right to left for a right side (knit) row, and left to right for a wrong side (purl) row. Use the Fairisle method for stranding the yarn across the chart. For neatness, we recommend knitting the first and last stitches of each row to ensure your coasters sit flat.

KEY

 Muker 367 (A)

☐ Buckden 364 (B)

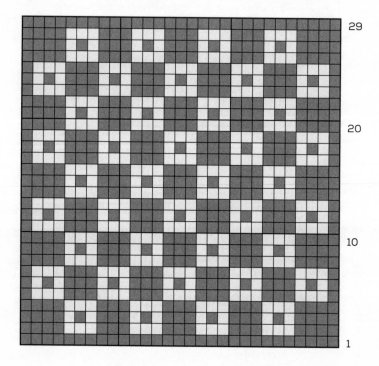

little colour knits

coaster

Using 3.25mm (US 3) needles and yarn A, cast on 29 sts.

Beg with a knit row, using colour chart as a guide, work all rows of colour chart to complete coaster.

Cast off purlwise using yarn A.

making up

Block or press to size as preferred.

Sew in ends.

clematis bag

This pretty small bag (and its button) are embroidered with a twining clematis inspired by one of my sketches. Feel free to adapt it as you wish!

finished size
10cm/4in square base x 20cm/8in, plus handle

yarns
Rowan Fine Tweed
2 x 25g balls in Burnsall 375 (A)
1 ball in Muker 367 (B)

needles
Pair of 3.25mm (US 3) knitting needles
Pair of 3.5mm (US 4) double pointed needles (dpn)
3.25mm (US D/3) crochet hook

extras
Self-cover buttonmaking kit, approx 2.5cm/1in diameter
Fine embroidery threads in pale green, pale blue, pale pink and yellow
Embroidery needle
50cm/20in cord
Lining fabric

tension
26sts and 38 rows to 10cm/4in square worked in St st using 3.25mm (US 3) needles, *or size to obtain correct tension.*

abbreviations
See page 66

bag body
Using 3.25mm (US 3) needles and yarn A, cast on 102 sts.
Beg with a knit row, work in St st until work measures 20cm/8in, ending with RS facing for next row.
Work facing as foll:
Change to yarn B.
Next row Knit.
Next row (folding line) Knit.
Next row K24, cast off next 3 sts (buttonhole space), k47, cast off next 3 sts (buttonhole space), k23.
Next row P24, cast on 3 sts, p48, cast on 3 sts, p24.
Work 6 rows in St st ending with RS facing for next row.
Cast off knitwise.
Embroider clematis detail onto bag following the photograph (opposite).

base
Using 3.25 mm (US 3) needles and yarn A, cast on 27 sts.

Beg with a knit row, work in St st until base square measures 10cm/4in from cast-on edge, ending with RS facing for next row.
Cast off knitwise.

handle

Using 3.5mm (US 4) dpns and yarn B, cast on 6 sts.
Holding cord at back of work, knit a row. Without turning work, slide sts to right-hand end of needle, pull yarn tight across back of work and behind cord, and knit the next row. Cont in this way, creating a knitted tube around the cord, until handle measures 45cm/17½in.
Cast off.

making up

Cut lining to size using knitted body bag as a template, adding a 1.5cm/½in seam allowance on the short sides only. Cut lining to size using knitted base, allowing 1.5cm/½in seam allowance. Sew sides of lining together using the 1.5cm/½in seam allowance to form a tube. Pin and sew in base of lining using the 1.5cm/½in seam allowance. Sew sides of bag body together to form a tube using mattress stitch. Turn bag inside out, and position base in bottom of bag with the seam running down the centre back of the bag. Backstitch the base to secure. Pass ends of the handle through the buttonhole spaces created in the facing and secure

in place. Fold facing using folding line onto wrong side of bag. Place lining tube over knitted bag with wrong sides together and slip stitch lining in place, turn bag to right side. Using a 3.25mm (US D/3) crochet hook, make 20ch and secure loop on centre back seam. Cover button following instructions in kit and attach on opposite edge.

clematis bag

seedling cushion

The seedling sketch translates well in the DK version of *Wool Cotton* for this elegant small cushion.

finished size
Approx 30 x 30cm/12 x 12in

yarns
Rowan *Wool Cotton*
2 x 50g balls in Antique 900 (A)
1 ball each in Ship Shape 955 (B),
Elf 946 (C), Rich 911 (D)

needles
Pair of 4mm (US 6) knitting needles

extras
Cushion back
30cm/12in cushion pad

tension
24 sts and 32 rows to 10cm/4in square measured over St st using 4mm (US 6) needles, *or size to obtain correct tension.*

abbreviations
See page 66

note
Chart is read from right to left for a right side (knit) row, and left to right for a wrong side (purl) row. Use the intarsia method for working the seedling patterns and grids across the chart.

cushion front
Using 4mm (US 6) needles and yarn A, cast on 77 sts. Now, using colour chart as a guide, work all rows of colour chart to complete cushion front.
Cast off.

making up
Block or press your cushion front as preferred, and sew in ends. With right sides together, sew cushion front and back together, remembering to insert the cushion pad before completing the fourth side if your back does not contain a zip.

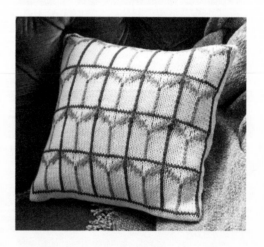

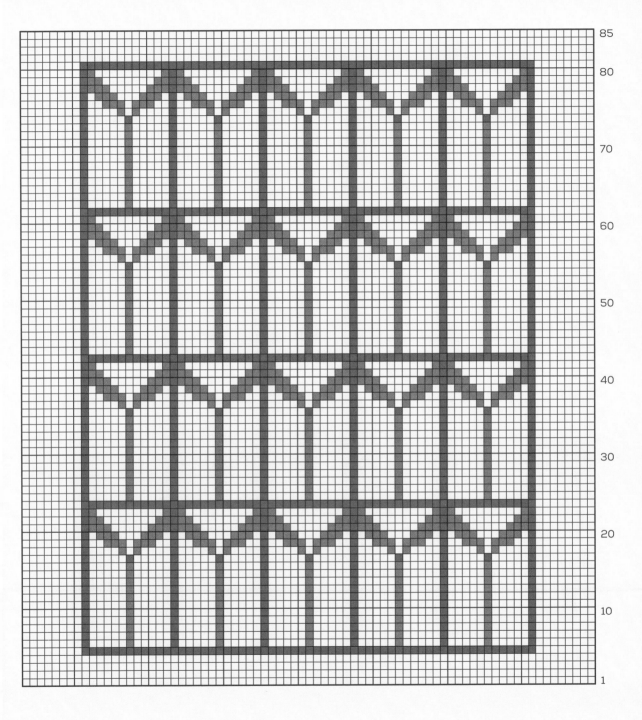

seedling cushion

KEY

☐ Antique 900 (A)   ▦ Elf 946 (C)

▦ Ship Shape 955 (B)   ▦ Rich 911 (D)

tulip lace wrap and hat

This little hat and wrap, inspired by a tulip design worked into a lace pattern and knitted in *Baby Merino Silk DK*, make great winter accessories.

tulip lace wrap

finished size
Approx 40 x 160cm/15½ x 63in

yarn
6 x 50g balls Rowan *Baby Merino Silk DK* in Strawberry (687)

needles
Pair of 4mm (US 6) knitting needles

tension
22sts and 30 rows to 10cm/4in square measured over St st using 4mm (US 6) needles, *or size to obtain correct tension.*

abbreviations
See page 66

shawl
Using 4mm (US 6) needles, cast on 88 sts.
1st row (RS) K1, *yf, k2tog, rep from * to last st, k1.
2nd row (WS) K1, purl to last st, k1.

tulip pattern
Row 1 K1, *yf, k2tog, k15, rep from * to last 2 sts, yf, k2tog.
Next and each alt row to row 26 K1, purl to last st, k1.
Row 3 K1, *yf, k2tog, k15, rep from * to last 2 sts, yf, k2tog.
Row 5 K1, *yf, k2tog, k7, yf, k2tog, k6, rep from * to last 2 sts, yf, k2tog.
Row 7 K1, *yf, k2tog, k7, yf, k2tog, k6, rep from * to last 2 sts, yf, k2tog.
Row 9 K1, *yf, k2tog, k7, yf, k2tog, k6, rep from * to last 2 sts, yf, k2tog.
Row 11 K1, *yf, k2tog, k7, yf, k2tog, k6, rep from * to last 2 sts, yf, k2tog.
Row 13 K1, *yf, k2tog, k7, yf, k2tog, k6, rep from * to last 2 sts, yf, k2tog.
Row 15 K1, *yf, k2tog, k7, yf, k2tog, k6, rep from * to last 2 sts, yf, k2tog.
Row 17 K1, *yf, k2tog, k6, [yf, k2tog] twice, k5, rep from * to last 2 sts, yf, k2tog.
Row 19 K1, *yf, k2tog, k5, [yf, k2tog] 3 times, k4, rep from * to last 2 sts, yf, k2tog.
Row 21 K1, *yf, k2tog, k4, [yf, k2tog] 4 times, k3, rep from * to last 2 sts, yf, k2tog.
Row 23 K1, *yf, k2tog, k7, yf, k2tog, k6, rep from * to last 2 sts, yf, k2tog.
Row 25 K1, *yf, k2tog, k15, rep from * to last 2 sts, yf, k2tog.
Row 27 K1, * yf, k2tog, k15, rep from * to last 2 sts, yf, k2tog.
Row 28 K1, *yrn, p2tog, rep from * to last st, k1.
These 28 rows complete tulip pattern repeat. Rep rows 1–28 16 times more.
Next row Cast off knitwise.

making up
Block or press as preferred. Sew in ends.

tulip lace hat

finished size

To fit head circumference small/ medium (medium/large): 62cm/24½in (66cm/26in)

yarns

2 x 50g balls Rowan *Baby Merino Silk DK* in Strawberry 687

needles

Pair of 4mm (US 6) knitting needles

extras

Stitch holder

tension

22sts and 30 rows to 10cm/4in square measured over St st using 4mm (US 6) needles, *or size to obtain correct tension.*

abbreviations

See page 66

hat band

Using 4mm (US 6) needles, cast on 21sts.
Row 1 K1, *yf, k2tog, rep from * to end.
Next and each alt row to to row 24 Purl.
Row 3 K1, yf, k2tog, k15, yf, k2tog, k1.
Row 5 K1, yf, k2tog, k7, yf, k2tog, k6, yf, k2tog, k1.
Row 7 K1, yf, k2tog, k7, yf, k2tog, k6, yf, k2tog, k1.
Row 9 K1, yf, k2tog, k7, yf, k2tog, k6, yf, k2tog, k1.
Row 11 K1, yf, k2tog, k7, yf, k2tog, k6, yf, k2tog, k1.
Row 13 K1, yf, k2tog, k6 [yf, k2tog] twice, k5, yf, k2tog, k1.
Row 15 K1, yf, k2tog, k5, [yf, k2tog] 3 times, k4, yf, k2tog, k1.
Row 17 K1, yf, k2tog, k4 [yf, k2tog] 4 times, k3, yf, k2tog, k1.
Row 19 K1, yf, k2tog, k7, yf, k2tog, k6, yf, k2tog, k1.
Row 21 K1, yf, k2tog, k15, yf, k2tog, k1.
Row 23 K1, yf, k2tog, k15, yf, k2tog, k1.
Row 25 *K3, p2, rep from * to last st, k1.
Row 26 K1, *k2, p3, rep from * to end.
These last 2 rows form rib. Rep these 2 rows until 139(147) rows of ribbing have been worked. Break off yarn, leaving 21 sts on a holder.

hat body

With RS facing, and beg at last row of ribbing, pick up and knit 138(146) sts along side edge of hat band, ending at first row of rib leaving first 24 rows of hat band free.
Purl one row.
Row 1 K1, *yf, k2tog, rep from * to last st, k1.
Next and each alt row to row 24 Purl.
Row 3 K1, [yf, k2tog, k15(16)] 8 times, k1.
Row 5 K1, [yf, k2tog, k15(16)] 8 times, k1.
Row 7 K1, [yf, k2tog, k7, yf, k2tog, k6(7)] 8 times, k1.
Row 9 K1, [yf, (k2tog) twice, k5, yf, k2tog,

k4(5), k2tog] 8 times, k1. (122(130) sts)

Row 11 K1, [yf, k2tog, k6, yf, k2tog, k5(6)] 8 times, k1.

Row 13 As row 11.

Row 15 K1, [yf, k2tog, k5, (yf, k2tog) twice, k4(5)] 8 times, k1.

Row 17 K1, [yf, (k2tog) twice, k2, (yf, k2tog) 3 times, k1(2), k2tog] 8 times, k1. (106(114) sts)

Row 19 K1, [yf, k2tog, k2 (yf, k2tog) 4 times, k1(2)] 8 times, k1.

Row 21 K1, [yf, k2tog, k5, yf, k2tog, k4(5)] 8 times, k1.

Row 23 K1, [yf, k2tog, k11(12)] 8 times, k1.

Row 25 K1, [yf, (k2tog) twice, k7(8), k2tog] 8 times, k1. (90(98) sts)

Row 26 P1 *yf, p2tog, rep from * to last st, p1.

Shape crown

Row 1 K1, [k9(10), ssk] 8 times, k1. (82(90) sts)

Row 2 P1, [p2tog tbl, p8(9)] 8 times, p1. (74(82) sts)

Row 3 K1, [k7(8), ssk] 8 times, k1. (66(74) sts)

Row 4 P1, [p2tog tbl, p6(7)] 8 times, p1. (58(66) sts)

Row 5 K1, [k5(6), ssk] 8 times, k1. (50(58) sts)

Row 6 P1, [p2tog tbl, p4(5)] 8 times, p1. (42(50) sts)

Row 7 K1, [k3(4), ssk] 8 times, k1. (34(42) sts)

Row 8 P1, [p2tog tbl, p2(3)] 8 times, p1.

(26(34) sts)

Row 9 K1, [k1(2), ssk] 8 times, k1. (18(26) sts)

First size only

Row 10 P1, [p2tog tbl] 8 times, p1. (10 sts)

Row 11 K1, [ssk] 4 times, k1. (6 sts)

Break off yarn, leaving a 30cm/12in length. Draw up through remaining 6 sts and secure to complete crown.

Second size only

Row 10 P1, [p2tog tbl] 8 times, p1. (18 sts)

Row 11 K1, [ssk] 8 times, k1. (10 sts)

Row 12 P1, [p2tog tbl] 4 times, p1. (6 sts)

Break off yarn, leaving a 30cm/12in length. Draw up through remaining 6 sts and secure to complete crown.

making up

Using mattress stitch or backstitch, if preferred, sew side seam of hat from crown to beginning of hat band and secure. With right side facing, pick up and knit 21 sts along free left-hand edge of hat band tulip tile. Now, with right sides together and holding this tile against the 21 sts remaining on the needle holder, use the three-needle cast off method to join and cast off the end of the hat band with the side of the hat band tulip tile. Sew in ends.

tulip lace tea cosy

I drink a lot of tea and a little cosy in my tulip lace pattern, worked in Rowan *Felted Tweed DK*, is both pretty and practical.

finished size

Approx 24 x 18cm/9½ x 7in, when flat

yarn

1 x 50g ball Rowan *Felted Tweed DK* in Rage 150

needles

Pair of 4mm (US 6) knitting needles
4mm (US F/5) crochet hook

extras

Stitch holder
1 button

tension

22sts and 30 rows to 10cm/4in square measured over St st patt using 4mm (US 6) needles, *or size to obtain correct tension.*

abbreviations

See page 66

tea cosy body (make 2)

Using 4mm (US 6) needles, cast on 54 sts
Row 1 K1, *yf, k2tog, rep from * to last st, k1.
Next and each alt row Purl.
Row 3 K1, *yf, k2tog, k15, rep from * to last 2 sts, yf, k2tog.
Row 5 K1, *yf, k2tog, k7, yf, k2tog, k6, rep from * to last 2 sts, yf, k2tog.
Row 7 K1, *yf, k2tog, k7, yf, k2tog, k6, rep from * to last 2 sts, yf, k2tog.
Row 9 K1, *yf, k2tog, k7, yf, k2tog, k6, rep from * to last 2 sts, yf, k2tog.

Row 11 K1, *yf, k2tog, k7, yf, k2tog, k6, rep from * to last 2 sts, yf, k2tog.
Row 13 K1, *yf, k2tog, k7, yf, k2tog, k6, rep from * to last 2 sts, yf, k2tog.
Row 15 K1, *yf, k2tog, k7, yf, k2tog, k6, rep from * to last 2 sts, yf, k2tog.
Row 17 K1, *yf, k2tog, k7, yf, k2tog, k6, rep from * to last 2 sts, yf, k2tog.
Row 19 K1, *yf, k2tog twice, k4 [yf, k2tog] twice, k5, rep from * to last 2 sts, yf, k2tog. (51 sts)
Row 21 K1, *yf, k2tog, k4, [yf, k2tog] 3 times, k4, rep from * to last 2 sts, yf, k2tog.
Row 23 K1, *yf, k2tog, k3, [yf, k2tog] 4 times, k3, repfrom * to last 2 sts, yf, k2tog.
Row 25 K1, *yf, k2tog, k6, yf, k2tog, k4, k2tog, rep from * to last 2 sts, yf, k2tog. (48 sts)
Row 27 K1, *yf, k2tog, k13, rep from * to last 2 sts, yf, k2tog.
Row 29 K1, *yf, k2tog, k6, k2tog, k5, rep from * to last 2 sts, yf, k2tog. (45 sts)
Row 31 K1, *yf, k2tog, rep from * to end.
Row 32 Purl.
Work 5 rows in St st, dec 1 st at each end of next and foll 4th row. (41 sts)
Leave remaining sts on a holder and complete 2nd body.

Joining pieces

Next row with WS facing, p40 sts from one body, purl last st of this body with 1 st of other body, purl to end. (81 sts)

tulip lace tea cosy

Shape top

Row 1 K1, *yf, k3tog, yf, k2tog, rep from * to end. (65 sts)

Next and each alt row Purl.

Row 3 K1, *k2tog, k5, rep from * to last st, k1. (56 sts)

Row 5 K1, *k2tog, k4, rep from * to last st, k1. (47 sts)

Row 7 K1, *k2tog, k3, rep from * to last st, k1. (38 sts)

Row 9 K1, *k2tog, k2, rep from * to last st, k1. (29 sts)

Row 11 K1, *k2tog, k1, rep from * to last st, k1. (20 sts)

Row 13 K1, [k2tog] 9 times, k1. (11 sts)

Row 14 Purl.

Break off yarn leaving a 30cm/12in length. Thread onto a yarn needle, draw through remaining sts and pull up. Using remaining length, use mattress stitch to join both bodies together for approx 6cm/2¼in from this centre circle.

making up

Flatten tea cosy so that the seam you have just completed is at the right-hand side of the tea cosy. We'll call this the handle seam, and the left-hand side the spout seam. For ease of description, I will refer to the body piece facing you as the **front** and the underside piece the **back**. Turn the whole tea cosy over and, using a small length of yarn and a 4mm (US F/5) crochet hook, make 12ch in the left-hand corner hole at the bottom of the **back** body. Work this back into the hole to create a button loop. Turn the cosy over so that the **front** piece is facing you again, and sew the button onto the right-hand corner at the bottom of the **front** body. Turn the tea cosy inside out, and join the **front** and **back** sections of the spout seam for approx 2cm/¾in from the cast-on edge. Sew in ends.

tulip wristwarmers

For these wristwarmers, I drew my inspiration directly from my tile designs. I love the geometric shapes and the use of colour.

finished size
Small/medium (medium/large)
Small/medium: approx 10 x 25cm/
4 x 10in, when flat
Medium/large: approx 11 x 25cm/
4¼ x 10in, when flat

yarns
Rowan Fine Tweed
3 x 25g balls in Bainbridge 369 (A)
2 balls in Richmond 381 (B)
1 ball each in Buckden 364 (C) and Nidd
382 (D)

needles
Pair of 3.25mm (US 3) knitting needles

extras
Stitch markers
4 buttons

tension
26 sts and 38 rows to 10cm/4in square
measured over St st using 3.25mm
(US 3) needles, *or size to obtain correct
tension.*

abbreviations
See page 66

note

Chart is read from right to left for a right side (knit) row, and left to right for a wrong side (purl) row. Use the intarsia method for working the tulip patterns and grids across the chart.

left glove

*Using 3.25mm (US 3) needles and yarn A, cast on 50(56) sts.
Beg with a knit row, work in St st for 25 rows, ending with WS facing for next row.
Next row (WS) Knit.
Beg with a knit row, work in St st for a further 25 rows, ending with WS facing for next row.
Next row (WS) Knit.
Changing to yarn B and beg at row 1 of the appropriate chart, work entire chart in St st using the intarsia method, ending with WS facing for next row.
Change to yarn A and purl 3 rows.
Cont in St st as foll:
Next row (RS) K14(17), place marker, m1, knit until 14(17) sts remain, m1, place marker, knit to end. (52(58) sts)
Work 3 rows.
Next row (RS) Knit to marker, slip marker, m1, knit to marker, m1, slip marker, knit to end. (54(60) sts)
Work 3 rows.
Next row (RS) Knit to marker, slip marker, m1, knit to marker, m1, slip marker, knit to end. (56(62) sts)
Next row Purl.**

Thumb shaping

Next row K8(10), cast off 15(18) sts, removing marker, and knit to end. (41(44) sts)
Next row Purl all sts up to cast off sts from previous row. Cast on 9(12) sts, join to rem sts and purl to end of row. (50(56) sts)
Beg with a knit row, work 11 rows in St st.
Next row (WS) Knit.
Starting with a knit row, work 10 rows in St st, ending with right side facing for next row.
Next row K8(10), cast off 9(12) sts, knit to end. (41(44) sts)
Next row Purl all sts up to cast off sts from previous row. Cast on 15(18) sts, join to rem sts and purl to end. (56(62) sts)
Next row K14(17), place marker, knit to last 14(17) sts, place marker, knit to end.
Next row Purl.
Dec row (RS) Knit to marker, slip marker, sl 1, k1, psso, knit to 2 sts before marker, k2tog, slip marker, knit to end. (54(60) sts)
Work 3 rows.
Dec row (RS) Knit to marker, slip marker, sl 1, k1, psso, knit to 2 sts before marker, k2tog, slip marker, knit to end. (52(58) sts)
Work 2 rows.
Next row Purl to marker, remove marker, p2tog, purl to 2 sts before marker, p2tog, remove marker, purl to end. (50(56) sts)
Complete according to making up instructions.

right glove

Work as given for left glove from * to **.

Next row K33(34), cast off 15(18) sts, removing marker and knit to end. (41(44) sts)

Next row Purl all sts up to cast-off sts from the previous row. Cast on 9(12) sts, join to rem sts and purl rest of row. (50(56) sts)

Beg with a knit row, work 11 rows in St st.

Next row (WS) Knit.

Starting with a knit row, work 10 rows in St st, ending with right side facing for next row.

Next row (RS) K33(34), cast off 9(12) sts, knit to end of row. (41(44) sts)

Next row (WS) Purl to start of cast-off sts from previous row, cast on 15(18) sts, turn and join to rem sts and purl to end of row. (56(62) sts)

Next row K14(17), place marker, knit to last 14(17) sts, place marker, knit to end.

Next row Purl.

Dec row (RS) Knit to marker, slip marker, sl 1, k1, psso, knit to 2 sts before marker, k2tog, slip marker, knit to end. (54(60) sts)

Work 3 rows.

Dec row (RS) Knit to marker, slip marker, sl 1, k1, psso, knit to 2 sts before marker, k2tog, slip marker, knit to end. (52(58) sts)

Work 2 rows.

Purl to marker, remove marker, p2tog, purl to 2 sts before marker, p2tog, remove marker, purl to end. (50(56) sts)

making up

Leaving sts on the needle before working, fold top red band in half on garter st fold line and graft single sts to the adjacent st on the red/green join, and repeat to graft all 50(56) sts.

Repeat the grafting at the bottom cuff to graft the cast-on edge to the red/green join row.

Use mattress stitch to sew the sides together, matching grey horizontal line.

Use slip stitch on outside of cuff and around to the inside of cuff and to the cast-on edge.

Weave in all intarsia loose ends.

Sew on buttons.

SMALL/MEDIUM SIZE CHART

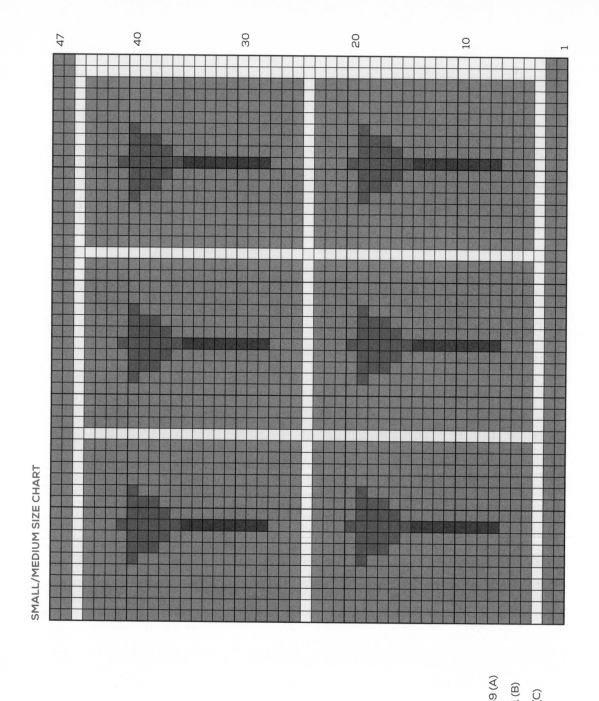

little colour knits

KEY

■ Bainbridge 369 (A)
■ Richmond 381 (B)
□ Buckden 364 (C)
■ Nidd 382 (D)

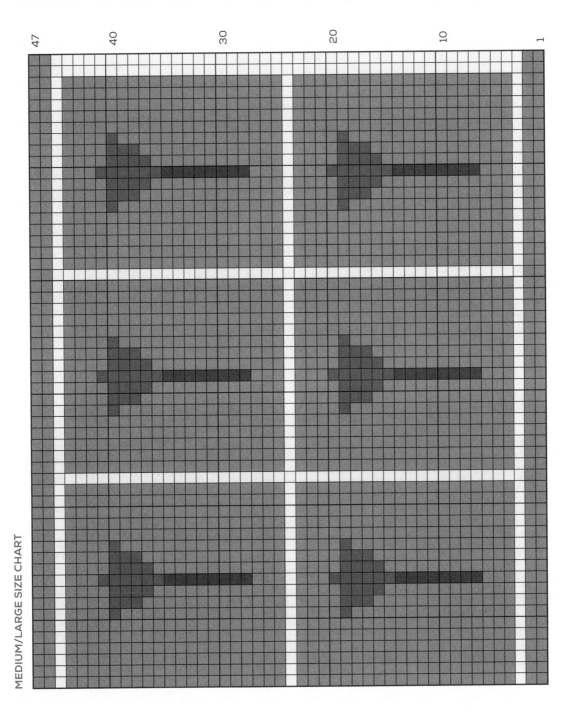

tulip wristwarmers

creating modular designs

If you wish, you could use the motifs in this book to create your own modular cushion or throw. For example, individual butterfly motifs (right), could be teamed checkerboard motifs (below) and perhaps block colour modules, too. Nine patches of alternating butterfly and checkerboards measure approx 26 x 26cm/10¼ x 10¼ in. A small throw (measuring 150 x 300cm/59 x 118in) would need 18 x 36 patches. Block colour modules would simply be 23-st x 24-row patches worked to complement the butterfly and checkerboard motifs.

To gauge the size and yarn required, make up one patch in each chosen colourway and multiply up the patch dimensions and yarn quantities accordingly. You can then work out how many modules and how much yarn you will need to make a throw or cushion of your desired size. If you are making a knitted cushion back, you will need an extra ball of yarn in your chosen colour to work a back to the required size.

If you wanted to add a border to the throw, you could create a 4- to 6-row garter stitch band, either by picking up stitches along the outer edges once all the squares have been stitched together, or by knitting a separate narrow border and stitching it to the patched and stitched throw.

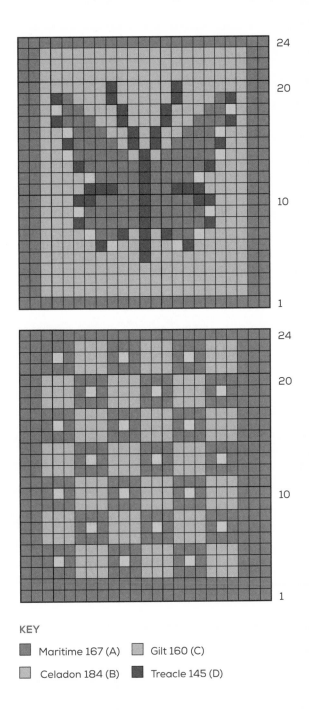

KEY

■ Maritime 167 (A)   □ Gilt 160 (C)

□ Celadon 184 (B)   ■ Treacle 145 (D)

creating modular designs

useful information

tension

To achieve the measurements given in the pattern, you must match the tension given at the start of each pattern. To check your tension, knit a square in the pattern stitch and/or stocking stitch of perhaps 5–10 more stitches and 5–10 more rows than those given in the tension note. Press the finished square under a damp cloth and mark out the central 10cm/4in square with pins. If you have too many stitches to 10cm/4in, try again using thicker needles. If you have too few stitches to 10cm/4in, try again using finer needles.

finishing instructions

Pressing

Block out each piece of knitting by pinning it on a board to the correct measurements in the pattern. Then lightly press it according to the ball band instructions, omitting any ribbed areas. Take special care to press the edges, as this makes sewing up easier and neater. If you cannot press the fabric, then cover the knitted fabric with a damp cloth and allow it to stand for a couple of hours. Darn in all ends neatly along the selvedge edge or a colour join, as appropriate.

Stitching seams

When you stitch the pieces together, remember to match any areas of colour and texture carefully where they meet. Use a special seam stitch, called mattress stitch, as it creates the neatest flattest seam. After all the seams are complete, press the seams and hems. Lastly, sew on the buttons to correspond with the positions of the buttonholes.

abbreviations

alt	alternate
approx	approximate
beg	begin(s)(ning)
ch	chain
cm	centimetres
cont	continu(e)(ing)
dec	decreas(e)(ing)
dpn	double pointed needle
foll	follow(s)(ing)
in	inch(es)
inc	increas(e)(ing)
k	knit
k2tog	knit next 2 stitches together
m	metre(s)
m1	make one stitch by picking up horizontal loop before next stitch and knitting into back of it
mm	millimetres
p	purl
patt	pattern
psso	pass slipped stitch over
p2tog	purl next 2 stitches together
rem	remain(s)(ing)
rep	repeat
rev St st	reverse stocking stitch
RS	right side
sl 1	slip one stitch
ssk	slip, slip, knit
st(s)	stitch(es)
St st	stocking stitch (1 row K, 1 row P)
tbl	through back of loop(s)
tog	together
WS	wrong side
yd	yard(s)
yf	yarn forward
yo(s)	yarn over(s)
yrn	yarn round needle

stockists

U.K.
Rowan, Green Lane Mill,
Holmfirth,
West Yorkshire HD9 2DX
www.knitrowan.com

U.S.A.
Westminster Fibers Inc,
8 Shelter Drive, Greer
South Carolina 29650
www.westminsterfibers.com

AUSTRALIA
Australian Country Spinners Pty Ltd,
Melbourne, Victoria 3004
Email: tkohut@auspinners.com.au

AUSTRIA
Coats Harlander Ges GmbH
1210 Vienna
www.coatscrafts.at

BELGIUM
See Germany

BULGARIA
Coats Bulgaria,
BG-1784 Sofia
www.coatsbulgaria.bg

CANADA
Westminster Fibers Inc,
Vaughan, Ontario L4H 3M8
www.westminsterfibers.coom

CHINA
Coats Shanghai Ltd, Shanghai
Email: victor.li@coats.com

CYPRUS
See Bulgaria

DENMARK
Coats Expotex AB, Dalsjöfors
Email: info.dk@coats.com

FINLAND
Coats Opti Crafts Oy, Kerava
04200
wwwcoatscrafts.fi

FRANCE
www.coatscrafts.fr

GERMANY
Coats GmbH, Kenzingen 79341
www.coatsgmbh.de

GREECE
See Bulgaria

HONG KONG
East Unity Company Ltd, Chai Wan
Email: eastunityco@yahoo.com.hk

ICELAND
Rowan At Storkurinn, Reykjavik 101
www.storkurinn.is

ITALY
Coats Cucirini srl, Milan 20126
www.coatscucirini.com

KOREA
Coats Korea Co. Lt, Seoul 137-060
www.coatskorea.co.kr

LEBANON
y.knot, Saifi Village, Beirut
Email: y.knot@cyberia.net.lb

LITHUANIA & RUSSIA
Coats Lietuva UAB, Vilnius 09310
www.coatscrafts.lt

LUXEMBOURG
See Germany

NEW ZEALAND
ACS New Zealand, Christchurch
Tel: 64 3 323 6665

NORWAY
Coats Knappehuset AS,
Bergen 5873
Email: kundeservice@coats.com

PORTUGAL
Coats & Clark,
Vila Nova de Gaia 4400
Tel: 351 223 770700

SINGAPORE
Golden Dragon Store,
Singapore 058357
Email: gdscraft@hotmail.com

SOUTH AFRICA
Arthur Bales Ltd,
Johannesburg 2195
Email: arthurb@new.co.za

SPAIN
Coats Fabra, Barcelona 08030
www.coatscrafts.es

SWEDEN
Coats Expotex AB
Email: kundtjanst@coats.com

SWITZERLAND
Coats Stroppel AG,
Untersiggenthal 5417
www.coatscrafts.ch

TAIWAN
Cactus Quality Co Ltd,
Taiwan, R.O.C. 10084
Tel: 00886-2-23656527

THAILAND
Global Wide Trading,
Bangkok 10310
Email: global.wide@yahoo.com

For stockists in all other countries
please contact Rowan for details

yarn information

The following are the specifications of the Rowan yarns used for the designs in this book. It is always best to try to obtain the exact yarns specified in the patterns, but when substituting yarns, remember to calculate the yarn amount needed by the meterage/yardage rather than by the ball weight. For yarn care directions, refer to the yarn label.

Rowan *Baby Merino Silk DK*
A superwash wool/silk mix yarn (66 per cent superwash wool/34 per cent silk): 50g/1¾oz (135m/147yd) per ball. Recommended tension: 22 sts and 30 rows to 10cm/4in measured over St st using 4mm (US 6) knitting needles.

Rowan *Felted Tweed DK*
A merino wool/alpaca/viscose mix yarn (50 per cent merino wool/25 per cent alpaca/ 25 per cent viscose); 50g/1¾oz (175m/191yd) per ball. Recommended tension: 22–24 sts and 30–32 rows to 10cm/4in measured over St st using 3.75–4mm (US 5–6) knitting needles.

Rowan *Fine Lace*
A baby alpaca/merino wool yarn (80 per cent baby alpaca/20 per cent merino wool); 50g/1¾oz (400m/437yd) per ball. Recommended tension: 20–39 sts and 33–54 rows to 10cm/4in measured over St st using 2–4mm (US 0–6) knitting needles.

Rowan *Fine Tweed*
A 100 per cent pure wool; 25g (approx 90m/98yd) per ball. Recommended tension: 26.5 sts and 38 rows to 10cm/4in measured over St st using 3.25mm (US 3) knitting needles.

Rowan *Lima*
A sportweight baby alpaca/merino wool/nylon mix yarn (84 per cent baby alpaca/8 per cent merino/8 per cent nylon); 50g/1¾oz (approx 100m/109yd) per ball. Recommended tension: 20 sts and 26 rows to 10cm/4in measured over St st using 5.5mm (US 9) knitting needles.

Rowan *Wool Cotton*
A sportweight wool/cotton mix yarn (50 per cent merino wool/50 per cent cotton); 50g/1¾oz (approx 113m/123yd) per ball. Recommended tension: 22–24 sts and 30–32 rows to 10cm/4in measured over St st using 3.25–4mm (US 5–6) knitting needles.

acknowledgments
Author's acknowledgments
With special thanks to Georgie Park without whose technical skills and lovely friendship this book could not have blossomed.
With special thanks to Ginevra at the Wool Croft for bringing us together.

Publisher's acknowledgments
The publishers would like to thank the following for their contribution to this book: Steven Wooster for photography, Anne Wilson for the design, Katie Hardwicke for editing, Georgina Park for pattern writing, Jill Gray for pattern checking and Dee Hardwicke and Sarah Tolner for locations.